D0468303

RECREATE DISCOVERIES ABOUT
LIVING THINGS

CRABTREE
PUBLISHING COMPANY
WWW.CRABTREEBOOKS.COM

ANNA CLAYBOURNE

RECREATE SCiENTiFiC DISCOVERIES

Author:
Anna Claybourne
Editorial director:
Kathy Middleton
Editors:
Sarah Silver
Sheri Doyle
Proofreader:
Heather Hewer
Interior design:
Eoin Norton & Katherine Berti
Cover design:
Katherine Berti
Photo research:
Diana Morris
Print and production coordinator:
Katherine Berti

Images:
All images by Eoin Norton for Wayland except the following:
A. Barrington Brown/SPL: p. 26tr
Dreamstime: Oleksandr Meinyk: p. 20tc
French Ministry of Culture and Communication, Rhône-Alpes region: p. 5b
Getty Images
    Antony Gormley. Figure, Another Place 2005/photo Sallycinnamon: p. 22cl
    David McNew: p. 29cr
    Johannes Simon/AFP: p. 22tr
    Stefano Bianchetti/Corbis: p. 14cl
    Ullsteinbild: p. 14tr
LOC: p. 16tr
© Numen/For Use. Photographer Aurélie Cenno: p. 18tr, 18cl
Shutterstock: front cover (fossil, stethoscope, flower, jar, fly,
    magnifying glass, stationery), p. 4br
    Attapol Yiemsiriwut: p. 13br
    Big Jamnong: p. 10tr
    Dora Zett: p. 5c
    Kletr: p. 15bl
    MriMAn: p. 4bl
    Naddya: p. 18tc
    Nejron Photo: p. 25bl
    NicholaS Piccillo: p. 9br
    Richard A McMillin: p. 5t
    Sabphoto: p. 17br
    Steve Crukov: p. 21cr
    Victoria Ki: p. 13bl
Superstock: Annie Owen/RobertHarding: p. 10cl
Wikimedia Commons: p. 6tr, 6tl, 8tr, 16cl
    Lyme Regis Museum: p. 28c
    PD: p. 28tr
    Rene-Theophile-Hyacinthe_Laennec: p. 20tr, 20cl
Every attempt has been made to clear copyright. Should there be any inadvertent omission please apply to the publisher for rectification.

Library and Archives Canada Cataloguing in Publication

Claybourne, Anna, author
    Recreate discoveries about living things /
Anna Claybourne.

(Recreate scientific discoveries)
Includes index.
Issued in print and electronic formats.
ISBN 978-0-7787-5053-6 (hardcover).--
ISBN 978-0-7787-5066-6 (softcover).--
ISBN 978-1-4271-2152-3 (HTML)

    1. Life sciences--Experiments--Juvenile literature. I. Title.

QH316.5.C532 2018   j570.78   C2018-902453-4
                                              C2018-902454-2

Library of Congress Cataloging-in-Publication Data

Names: Claybourne, Anna, author.
Title: Recreate discoveries about living things / Anna Claybourne.
Description: New York, New York : Crabtree Publishing Company, 2019. |
  Series: Recreate scientific discoveries | Includes index.
Identifiers: LCCN 2018021345 (print) | LCCN 2018022080 (ebook) |
  ISBN 9781427121523 (Electronic) |
  ISBN 9780778750536 (hardcover) |
  ISBN 9780778750666 (paperback)
Subjects: LCSH: Life sciences--Experiments--Juvenile literature.
Classification: LCC QH316.5 (ebook) | LCC QH316.5 .C53 2019 (print) |
  DDC 570.78--dc23
LC record available at https://lccn.loc.gov/2018021345

Crabtree Publishing Company
www.crabtreebooks.com   1-800-387-7650
Published in 2019 by Crabtree Publishing Company

Published in Canada
Crabtree Publishing
616 Welland Ave.
St. Catharines, Ontario
L2M 5V6

Published in the United States
Crabtree Publishing
PMB 59051
350 Fifth Avenue, 59th Floor
New York, New York 10118

Note:
In preparation of this book, all due care has been exercised with regard to the instructions, activities and techniques depicted. The publishers regret that they can accept no liability for any loss or injury sustained. Always follow the manufacturers' advice when using electric and battery-powered appliances.

The website addresses (URLs) included in this book were valid at the time of going to press. It is possible that some addresses may have changed or sites may have changed or closed down since publication. While the author and publishers regret any inconvenience this may cause to the readers, no responsibility for any such changes can be accepted by either the author or the publishers.

Printed in the U.S.A./082018/CG20180601

CONTENTS

4   **Understanding living things**

6   **Miniature plant world** | Science: plant life, ecosystems, water cycle

8   **Fast flowers** | Science: flowering plants, photography

10   **Natural tie-dye** | Science: plant pigments

14   **Close-up creepy crawlies** | Science: entomology

16   **Animal flip book** | Science: animal movement, animation

18   **Weave a web** | Science: spider webs

20   **Hear your heart** | Science: human body and heart, sound science

22   **Body copy** | Science: human body, casting materials

26   **Building blocks of life** | Science: genes and DNA

28   **Fabulous fossils** | Science: fossil formation, animal skeletons

30   **Glossary**

31   **Further information**

32   **Index**

TAKE CARE!

You can make these projects with materials and tools found at home, or in a grocery store, craft store, or hardware store. Some of the projects involve the use of sharp or breakable objects, or need extra strength to operate. Please get permission to do these projects, and make sure an adult is available to help

UNDERSTANDING LIVING THINGS

Life is all around us. Grass, trees, plants, **fungi**, **bacteria**, animals, and humans are living things. There are millions of different **species**, or types, of living things on our planet. Life has existed on Earth for billions of years.

We don't know exactly how or where life first began, but scientists have found that all living things are related. They all use the chemical **DNA**, found inside **cells**, as a way of storing and passing on information that controls how each species grows and survives.

All of the living things on Earth are related to the first life forms and are connected to each other in a huge family tree.

WHAT IS LIFE?

All living things take in food, grow, sense their surroundings, and make copies of themselves, or have babies. Living things are complex. Some living things, such as humans, are also intelligent and creative.

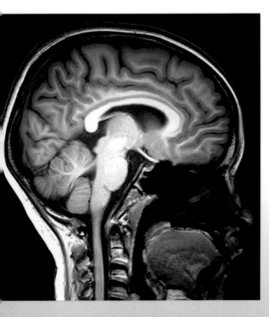

The human brain is a complex organ that is the control center for thought, the senses, the nervous system, and functions of the body.

We use the fluffy seed coverings of the cotton plant to make fabric for clothes.

THE SCIENCE OF LIFE

Biology is the study of living things. This means studying plants, animals, and **ecosystems** that we depend on for food. It is one of the most important aspects of science. The study of living things has led to useful inventions, such as farming, **breeding** animals, using plants to make cotton fabric, and making medicines to treat illnesses.

Humans have created many different dog breeds by breeding from a wild animal, the grey wolf.

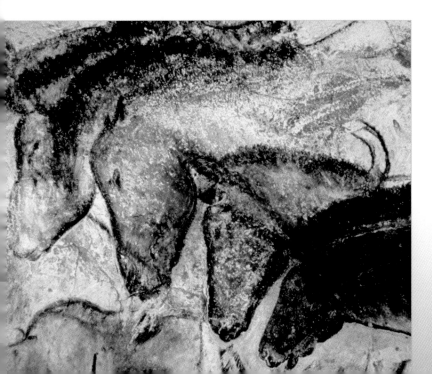

LIVING THINGS AND ART

Living things have inspired artists since ancient times. Most of the earliest known artworks are sculptures or cave paintings of animals. Artworks of the past and the present often feature flowers, trees, plants, animals, and humans. Some artists use living things in their creations. Others use film and photography to try to capture the beauty of life.

This cave drawing of horses, found in Lascaux, France, is 17,000 years old.

MINIATURE PLANT WORLD

Make your own terrarium—a tiny greenhouse that was invented accidentally by Nathaniel Bagshaw Ward.

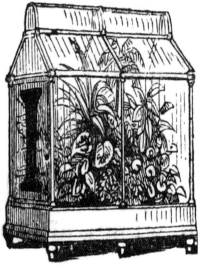

Victorian explorers used Wardian cases to transport tropical plants back to Britain on long sea journeys.

NATHANIEL BAGSHAW WARD

(1791–1868)

Nathaniel Bagshaw Ward was a doctor in London, England who studied plants and insects in his spare time. In 1829, Ward put a moth **pupa** and some soil into a jar, and put the lid on it. A few days later, he noticed plants growing in the soil. Ward realized that water had **evaporated**, meaning it moved up and became a gas. Then it **condensed**, meaning it changed back into water, and dripped down the sides of the jar—so the soil always stayed damp, and plants could live inside. Based on this, he invented the Wardian case, a mini-greenhouse called a **terrarium**.

WHAT YOU NEED

- a large, clear glass or plastic jar with a lid
- gravel or small stones
- activated charcoal (from a garden store or pet store)
- potting compost
- a jug of water
- a fork
- a spray bottle
- a small plant (or a few if your jar is large enough), such as a miniature violet, begonia, fern, or club moss

1

Step 1

Wash and dry your jar and lid. Add a layer of stones or gravel about 1 inch (2 cm) deep, then a layer of activated charcoal about 1 inch (2 cm) deep. Spread them out gently with the fork.

2

Step 2

Now add a layer of potting compost about 2 inches (5 cm) deep. Use the fork to level and pat down the compost, and to dig a hole for the plant.

3

Step 3

Before you put the plant in the hole, water it and let soak for a few minutes. Then remove it from its pot and plant it in the soil. Press down the compost around the plant with the fork.

4

Step 4

Fill the spray bottle with water and spray the plant, the compost and the sides of the jar with water several times each.

5

Step 5

Put the lid on and place the terrarium in a safe place where it will receive daylight, but not direct bright sunlight, which could overheat it. Check it each day, and add a little more water if it looks dry.

THE WATER CYCLE

A terrarium is like a mini ecosystem or mini planet Earth, with its own **water cycle**. The water evaporates into the air, then rises to the top, where it cools, condenses, and "rains" back down into the soil. As water moves around in this cycle, it passes through the soil and plants, helping them grow.

Plants also need a gas called **carbon dioxide**. They take it in from the air, then they let out **oxygen**. Meanwhile, bacteria in the soil release carbon dioxide and take in oxygen, helping to keep the plants alive. Opening the terrarium once every few days will also help to refresh the air inside.

FAST FLOWERS

Create an amazing movie of a flower opening up in fast motion.

WHAT YOU NEED

- fresh cut flower buds, such as irises, daffodils, or tulips
- scissors
- a glass or small vase
- warm water
- a smartphone with a time-lapse function (see note below)
- a tripod, or some books and adhesive putty

If your phone doesn't have a time-lapse function, you can use a time-lapse app, such as OSnap! or Hyperlapse. Choose one that will work with your phone, and follow the instructions to set it up to make a time-lapse movie over several hours.

JOHN OTT

(1909–2000)

John Ott was an American photographer who made early time-lapse films, which were movies in fast motion. Using his camera, he captured slow changes, such as a flower opening, so that he could watch these changes in fast motion. His photography started as a hobby, but it soon became his work as he designed and built cameras and special parts to photograph his greenhouses full of plants. He became famous for his work, which was used in several films. He also wrote books about his methods.

1

2

3 & 4

5

6

Step 1
For your film, choose flower buds that are starting to open and have some color showing. Cut off the bottoms of the stems at a sharp angle.

Step 2
Fill the glass or vase with warm (not hot) tap water and place the flowers in it. (This helps them open up faster.)

Step 3
Place the glass or vase in a safe spot under artificial light, such as a floor lamp or ceiling light, so that the lighting won't change too much. Set up your time-lapse function or app, but don't start it yet.

Step 4
Set up your phone on the tripod, pointing at the flowers. If you don't have a tripod, stand the phone up between two piles of books with strips of adhesive putty along the bottom to hold it in place.

Step 5
Keep checking the flowers until you see at least one of them just beginning to open. At this point, start the time-lapse function and begin filming.

Step 6
Leave the phone filming for as long as possible, or until the flower has fully opened (it may take several hours). The film should be stored just like a normal video, which you can then save, view, and share. Since it has far fewer frames than a normal video, it should not take up too much memory space.

FRAME BY FRAME

A normal movie or video is made of lots of separate photographs, or frames, taken several times per second. For a time-lapse movie, the camera shoots a frame much less often—for example, once every minute. Then it plays them back quickly, like a normal video. This speeds up something that happens very slowly in real life. Not only is it fascinating to watch, but time-lapse photography is also very useful—scientists can study things like plants, insect **life cycles**, and the growth of bacteria or **algae**.

NATURAL TIE-DYE

Use plant dyes from your fridge, cupboard, or grocery store to make amazing colors and patterns on fabric.

Natural products, such as indigo for blue (left) and dried flowers for yellow (above right), are still used to create dyes today.

ANCIENT INDIAN DYERS

(From c. 2500 BCE)

The ancient people of what is now India were famous for their skillful coloring of cloth with natural dyes. They used plants, such as **indigo**, **turmeric**, and madder to dye cloth. They also used animals, such as the lac insect. They described these natural dyes in ancient Indian writings, such as the Vedas. The Indian tradition of colorful dyeing continues today.

WHAT YOU NEED

Your fabric must fit inside the pan, so make sure your piece isn't too big. It should be the size of a tea towel, or smaller.

- a piece of plain white or cream 100 percent natural fabric, such as cotton or linen
- a large pot, such as a stockpot
- a measuring cup or jug
- table salt
- an old wooden spoon
- old newspapers

- a vegetable knife
- an old tea towel or pillowcase
- strong, thin string or extra-strength sewing thread
- scissors
- fruit, vegetables, or spices to dye with (see box on page 11)

1&2

3&4

Step 1

If your fabric is new, wash it in a washing machine before using it. This removes any chemicals or surface coatings that may have been added to it in the factory.

Step 2

With an adult's help, fill the pot with 8 cups (1.89 L) of hot tap water, and stir in a 1/2 cup (118 ml) of salt.

Step 3

Put the fabric into the salty water, and push it down with the spoon. Ask an adult to heat the pot on a stove. As soon as the water boils, turn down the burner to a lower setting so that the fabric simmers for an hour. Stir occasionally. This will help the fabric soak up the dye you will put in later. It's important to stay close-by and watch over the pot.

Step 4

After an hour, ask an adult to pour the hot water down a drain, leaving the fabric to cool, in the pot. Once cool, squeeze the water out of the fabric. Ask the adult to refill the pan with hot water and heat it up again until it boils.

5

Here are some of the plant dyes you could use, and the colors you might get from them:

Bay leaves—yellow
Beetroot—pinkish-purple
Blackberries—purple
Blueberries—
   bluish-purple
Brown onion skins—
   orange yellow
Cherries – pink
Red cabbage—
   bluish-purple
Red onion skins—pink
Spinach—green
Teabags—light brown
Turmeric powder—yellow

Step 5

With an adult's help, add one plant dye to the water, and let it simmer. For one pot of water, use a large handful of fruit or vegetables, or one package of turmeric. If you're using beetroot, ask an adult to chop it into small pieces.

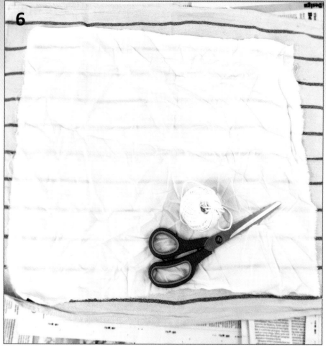

Step 6

Spread newspaper on a kitchen or bathroom floor, away from carpets. Lie an old tea towel or pillowcase on the newspaper, and spread out your damp fabric on top.

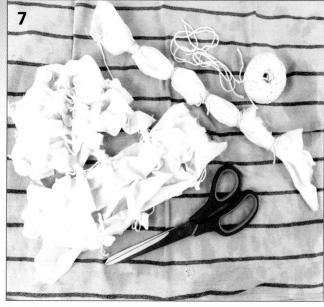

Step 7

Cut pieces of string about 6 to 12 inches (15 to 30 cm) long. Tie the strings around the fabric in different ways. For example, you could pinch or twist small pieces of the fabric and wrap thread tightly around them. You could also fold or crumple the whole piece of fabric and tie string tightly around it in sections.

Step 8

When your fabric is all tied up, ask an adult to lower it gently into the pot of hot dye, and push it under with the wooden spoon. Stir and turn over the fabric every few minutes.

Step 9

Simmer the fabric for at least another hour, staying close-by so you can watch over it. Then turn the heat off and leave the fabric in the pot until it has completely cooled down. Ask an adult to pour the water down a drain and throw out any pieces of plant material.

10

Rinse your fabric in water. Carefully snip off the pieces of string or thread, making sure you don't cut into the fabric. Spread out the fabric and rinse it again. Squeeze the water out of the fabric, then hang it up to dry.

Fabric dyed this way will not be completely colorfast, as this requires stronger chemicals—so avoid washing it in the washing machine. But you can use it to make things like bunting, a cushion cover, or a decoration for a bag.

PLANT PIGMENTS

Fruit, vegetables, flowers, and plants are often very colorful—but why? Plants contain **pigments**, or naturally colored substances, for many reasons. Plants use the green pigment called **chlorophyll** to take in energy from sunlight. The bright colors of berries help birds to see and eat them, and spread the eaten plants' seeds around in their droppings. Purplish pigments called **anthocyanins** are thought to help plants recover from damage. Chopping, crushing, and heating plant material helps to break down the plants so that they release the pigments. They can then soak into the fibers of a natural fabric, such as cotton.

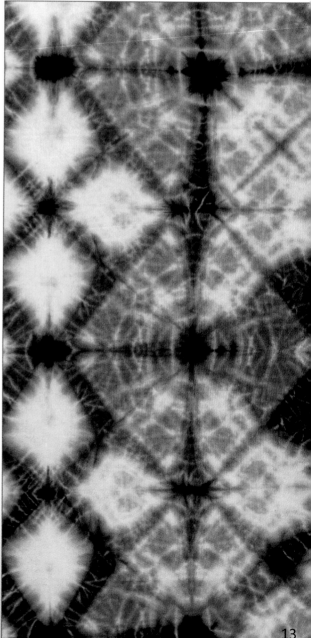

CLOSE-UP CREEPY CRAWLIES

We often ignore or even run away from insects. Instead, make a bug viewer and take a closer look!

Fabre's home is now a museum in Provence, France.

JEAN-HENRI FABRE

(1823–1915)

By the time he died at 91, Jean-Henri Fabre was renowned as a great **entomologist**, or insect scientist. Yet he was mostly self-taught, studying insects as a hobby while working as a teacher. For many years he was not taken seriously. At the time, most naturalists simply caught and killed insects and studied their bodies. Fabre preferred to work with living creatures to watch their behavior. He captured and watched insects safely using everyday objects, such as bowls, jars, and bottles.

> "You rip up the animal and I study it alive; you turn it into an object of horror and pity, whereas I cause it to be loved.
> – *Jean-Henri Fabre*

WHAT YOU NEED

- a clear plastic container with a thin, flexible plastic lid
- a plastic magnifying glass, or a magnifying **lens**, smaller than the lid
- a marker
- scissors or craft knife
- a strong glue or hot glue gun
- a large needle

1

2

3

4

5

6

Step 1
If you have a magnifying glass with a handle, ask an adult to remove the lens from the frame, or remove the handle, if possible. (If not, you can leave it on.)

Step 2
Place the magnifying glass lens on the middle of the container lid, and draw around it with the marker.

Step 3
To make a hole in the lid, ask an adult to cut just slightly inside the drawn circle using scissors or a craft knife.

Step 4
Ask an adult to use strong glue or a hot glue gun to put glue all around the edge of the hole. Stick the lens over the hole, making sure there are no gaps. Set aside to dry.

Step 5
Use the needle to make a ring of small air holes around the edge of the lid.

Step 6
Find an insect to view. Take the lid off the viewer and gently brush the insect into the container, or push it in with a piece of card. Press the lid back on and look through the lens. Once you've viewed the insect, set it free again.

CLOSE-UP

Insects are fascinating to look at, but it can be hard to see all the details because they're often so small. A magnifying lens has a curved surface that bends the light that comes from objects towards our eyes. The bent rays of light make the object appear to be much bigger than it is.

15

ANIMAL FLIP BOOK

Eadweard Muybridge wanted to find out how horses run, so he invented a way to capture every step and animate the images. Make an animal flip book to watch a horse in motion.

Muybridge used a zoopraxiscope and a glass picture disk to make a moving image.

EADWEARD MUYBRIDGE

(1830–1904)

Eadweard Muybridge was one of the first British photographers. In 1872, racehorse owner Leland Stanford asked Muybridge to use photography to find out whether horses completely left the ground as they ran (a popular debate at the time). Muybridge set up a row of cameras, each one triggered by a string stretched across a track. As a horse ran along it, the cameras photographed every stage of its movement. Muybridge also invented a device called the **zoopraxiscope**. It displayed the photographs quickly in order, creating a moving image.

> Only photography has been able to divide human life into a series of moments. Each of them has the value of a complete existence.
> – *Eadweard Muybridge*

WHAT YOU NEED

- a computer, printer, and paper
- scissors
- a small, thick notebook
- paper glue

16

1

Step 1

Find a good, clear image of *The Horse in Motion*, or another of Muybridge's animal movement sequences, on the Internet. Print it out, making the image as big as possible on the printer paper. One copy will work, but to make a longer flip book, you could print out extra copies.

2

Step 2

Cut out each frame in the printout, making sure you keep them all in the right order! If you have more than one printout, make each page into a separate pile of cut pictures.

3

Step 3

Take the first photograph and glue it into the first page of your notebook. Line it up with the outside edge of the page. Use only a small amount of glue to avoid making the page too heavy.

4

Step 4

Stick the next picture in the exact same place on the next page. Continue gluing the pictures in order on to the pages. After you finish the first pile, move on to the next until they are all used up or you run out of pages.

5

Step 5

Separate all the pages from each other in case any have stuck together. Let the glue dry completely. Then hold the book in your left hand, and flip through the pages with your right, to see the animal moving.

PUTTING IT TOGETHER

Film, video, and animated cartoons work by showing the viewer a series of still images in quick succession. Muybridge's zoopraxiscope did this too, and so does a flip book. This is different from real life, where things really do move continuously. Yet the viewer still sees the image "moving" in a realistic way.

It works because if the brain receives images of something in two different positions close together, it automatically "fills in" movement between them—making human and animal movements look lifelike and realistic on the screen. Scientists aren't sure how it works—but the whole film and TV industry relies on it!

Most movie projectors move the film at a speed of 24 frames per second.

WEAVE
A WEB

Learn how to spin your own web like the art team Numen/For Use.

Tape Hasselt, *House for Contemporary Art,* Hasselt, Belgium, 2012

NUMEN/ FOR USE

(Founded in 1999)

Numen/For Use is the name of a European art collective, or team. They work together to make large-scale art projects, often inspired by living things and the natural world. Among other artworks, they have created several huge webs made from tape or string and suspended them across gallery spaces, courtyards, rivers, and parks, as if left there by enormous spiders.

> "The first architecture ever made, by animals, is made the same way, like this."
> — *Sven Jonke*

WHAT YOU NEED

- a large ball of string or yarn
- scissors
- nails or screw-in hooks
- a hammer
- a place to attach your web to—it could be in the corner of a room inside, or between trees or fences outside

Step 1
Decide where you are going to put your web. You will need three or four anchor points—these are the places where you'll put nails or hooks in Step 2.

Step 2
Ask an adult to put nails or hooks into the walls or door frames to make the anchor points. (Make sure you get permission from the owner of the building.) If you're outdoors, you could tie the string or yarn around fence posts and tree branches instead.

Step 3
Unroll your string or yarn and tie the end firmly to one of your anchor points. Stretch it tightly to the next point, and tie or attach it there. Tie the string or yarn to your next chosen anchor point, and continue, until finally bringing it back to the point you started at. Tie the string there again, and snip off the rest.

Step 4
You should now have a large square, rectangle, or triangle shape. Cut lengths of string or yarn and tie them across the shape from one side to the other. They should all cross each other in the middle. Snip off the loose ends.

Step 5
Tie a long piece of string or yarn to the middle of the web. Now begin to curve the string around and around , working outwards. Each time you come to one of the strings, tie the thread around it. If you use up your string, tie another piece to it.

Step 6
When you reach the outer edge, tie a knot and snip the rest off.

SPIDER SCIENCE

The steps for building this spiral web are the same ones that spiders use. Spiders make webs to catch their prey. Unlike us, they don't have to learn how to spin a web. Spiders spin webs using **instinct**, which means it is an action they do naturally.

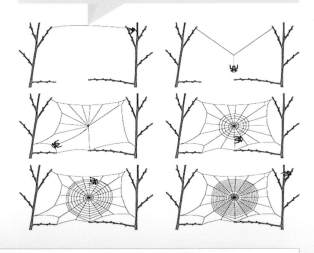

A web like this makes a great bedroom feature or party decoration. You could even make a rainbow web using string or yarn of different colors. Or try plastic wrap twisted into a thin rope—it is see-through and makes a slightly sticky web.

HEAR YOUR HEART

The stethoscope **is a simple listening device that helps doctors hear what's going on inside the human body. You can make a model of one and listen to your heart.**

RENÉ LAENNEC

(1781–1826)

In 1816, René Laennec was a busy doctor in a large hospital in Paris. One day, he was having problems checking a patient's heartbeat. He remembered that he'd recently seen children playing with wooden tubes, making noises at one end and listening at the other. So he rolled several sheets of paper into a tube, held one end to the woman's heart, and put his ear to the other. It worked! He heard the patient's heartbeat loud and clear. Following this discovery Laennec designed a simple hollow wooden tube with a listening piece at one end. He had invented the first version of the stethoscope, which gets its name from the Greek words for "chest-looking."

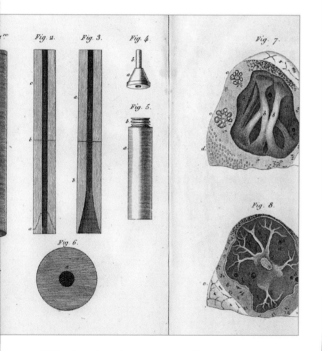

This drawing shows Laennec's basic stethoscope design.

> **"** I immediately saw that this might become an indispensable method for studying, not only the beating of the heart, but all movements able of producing sound in the chest cavity. **"**
> **– René Laennec**

WHAT YOU NEED

- about 18 inches (46 cm) of flexible plastic tubing from a hardware store
- two small funnels
- tape
- a watch or timer
- pen and paper

1

Step 1

Connect one end of the tubing to one of the funnels. If one doesn't fit inside the other, line them up and join them with tape. Do the same with the other funnel at the other end.

2

Step 2

Hold one funnel to your ear, and press the other against your chest just left of the middle. You should be able to hear your heart beating.

3

Step 3

To test your heart, sit still for a few minutes, then listen to your heartbeat. Use the watch or timer to count how many times your heart beats in 15 seconds.

For example, you might hear 20 beats in 15 seconds. Multiply this by 4 to give you your heart rate per minute. 20 x 4 = 80 beats per minute.

Try measuring your heartbeat before and after doing jumping jacks for 30 seconds. Is it different?

INTO YOUR EARS

Like other tube-shaped sound inventions, the stethoscope carries and directs **sound waves**. The sounds of the heart travel along the tube and into the ear. The stethoscope became even more effective when later inventors improved it, using flexible tubes that linked to both ears instead of one. Doctors still use the stethoscope today.

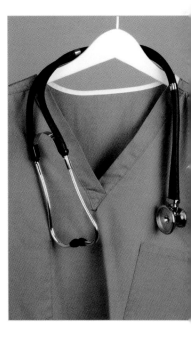

heart

lungs

stomach

intestines

As René Laennec realized, the stethoscope can be used to listen to other body parts too. You could use yours to try listening to your lungs, your stomach after a big meal, or your intestines.

21

BODY COPY

Sculptor Antony Gormley creates casts of his entire body. To learn more about how he makes a body copy, create a cast of your hand!

One of the body cast figures from Antony Gormley's work Another Place.

ANTONY GORMLEY

(1950–)

Sir Antony Gormley is a leading British sculptor who is best-known for using casts of his own body to make many of his works. The body-shaped sculptures have appeared in galleries, city streets, on top of buildings, on a beach, and in many other locations.

Gormley makes the casts by covering his body in plastic wrap to protect his skin, then two assistants coat him in plaster. This makes a mold which is used to cast the sculpture. Gormley often adds other parts and shapes, such as ridges, wings, or a surface texture.

WHAT YOU NEED

> "All the proportions that mean things to us as human beings are related to the body.
> *— Antony Gormley*

- old newspapers
- a large, empty plastic bottle
- a ruler
- a marker
- 1 pound (500g) of alginate powder (see below)
- strong scissors
- petroleum jelly or baby oil
- a mixing bowl or large plastic jug
- an electric hand-held mixer
- a measuring cup
- a wooden skewer
- plaster of Paris powder, a material found at craft and supply stores
- a large yogurt or ice cream tub that is empty and clean
- measuring cups

Alginate is a non-toxic, jelly-like molding material made from seaweed. It's easy to find in craft stores, art supply stores, or online. Any alginate that gets onto your hands, equipment, or kitchen surfaces will peel off easily once it's dry.

1&2

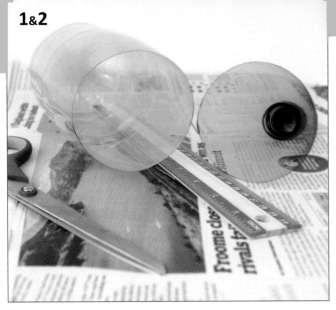

3

Step 1

Decide which hand you are going to make a cast of. Remove any jewelry or bandages, and wash and dry your hand. Spread out newspapers to work on.

Step 2

Measure about 10 inches (25 cm) up from the base of your plastic bottle, and mark a line there. With an adult's help, use the scissors to cut off the top of the bottle.

Step 3

Check the instructions on your alginate to find out how much water to add, and measure out the amount in your measuring cup. Tip the alginate powder into the mixing bowl. Ask an adult to plug in the electric mixer and have it ready.

4

5

Step 4

Rub a small amount of petroleum jelly or baby oil all over the hand you are going to cast, including a little way up the arm. Have the cut-off bottle ready too. You will need to do the next steps quite quickly, as the alginate sets in just a couple of minutes.

Step 5

Pour the water into the alginate powder and ask an adult to mix it well with the electric mixer for about 20 seconds. Then they should quickly pour the mixture into the cut-off bottle, filling it about three-quarters full.

Step 6

Put your hand into the alginate mixture in the bottle, and push it down so that the mixture comes up over your wrist. Keep the hand still in the position you want, making sure it doesn't push against the sides of the bottle. Wait two to three minutes for the mixture to set.

Step 7

Tap the top of the mixture to check it has set into a firm jelly. Then gently begin to wiggle your fingers and move your arm from side to side slightly, to let air into the space. Gradually and gently pull your hand out of the mold. Since the alginate is flexible, this is not difficult.

WARNING

Always have an adult with you when using plaster of Paris, and do not pour unused plaster down the sink! It will harden and clog the pipes. Leave it to harden in the yogurt or ice cream tub, then throw the tub away.

Step 8

Wash and dry your hand. Then measure out 1 cup of water into your yogurt or ice cream tub. Add 1.5 cups of plaster of Paris powder. Stir with the wooden skewer until the mixture is smooth and creamy.

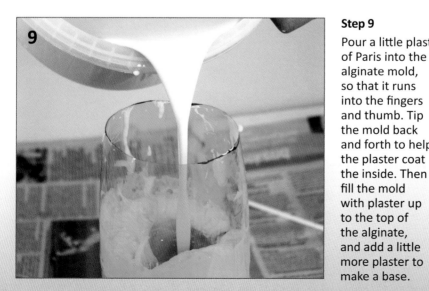

Step 9

Pour a little plaster of Paris into the alginate mold, so that it runs into the fingers and thumb. Tip the mold back and forth to help the plaster coat the inside. Then fill the mold with plaster up to the top of the alginate, and add a little more plaster to make a base.

Step 10

Leave the plaster to harden for several hours. Then you can carefully cut down the side of the bottle and remove the plastic.

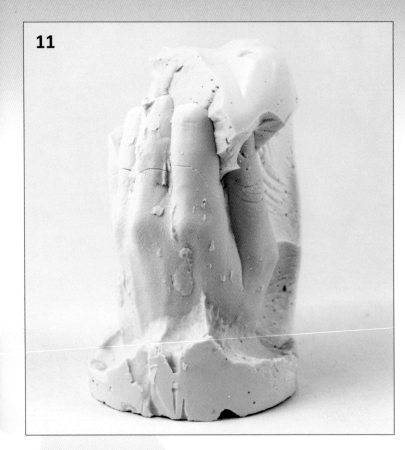

11

Step 11

Carefully peel and cut the rubbery alginate away from the plaster. Inside you will find a plaster cast of your hand.

> If the cast breaks or any fingers fall off, don't worry. Leave the parts a few more hours to dry out, then ask an adult to glue them back together with strong glue.

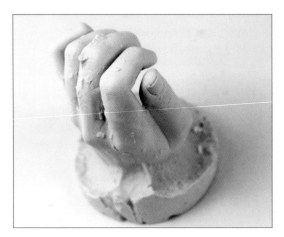

PERFECT COPIES

Casting is an ancient technique that has been used for thousands of years. By coating or covering an object with something soft that then sets, you can make a copy of it that picks up every tiny detail. Alginate is especially good for this. If you look closely at your hand cast, you should be able to see tiny wrinkles, and the texture of your skin.

For this reason, dentists use alginate to make casts of the inside of people's mouths. It's also used by special effects artists to make masks that will fit perfectly onto an actor's face.

> You could use your hand cast as a sculpture, a ring holder, or a scary decoration. When your cast is completely dry, it can be painted with acrylic or water-based paints. You can also make casts of your feet, in the same way, using a wider container.

BUILDING BLOCKS OF LIFE

DNA is a material found mostly inside our cells that controls how living things grow and work. Make your own model of DNA!

WHAT YOU NEED

- a long wooden skewer
- strong garden wire
- wire cutters
- a block of Styrofoam to use as a base
- small Styrofoam balls (from a craft or art supply store)
- scissors
- large wooden or plastic beads with large holes, all the same color
- several pipe cleaners, all the same color
- drinking straws in four different colors

JAMES WATSON

(left) (1928–)

FRANCIS CRICK

(right) (1916–2004)

Today, we know a lot about genes, and DNA, the chemical they are made from. But it took many years and many scientists to discover DNA and how it worked. In 1953, British biologist Francis Crick and his American colleague James Watson managed to figure out a key part of the puzzle—the shape of the DNA molecule. To help them, they built a model of it, showing its spiral-ladder-like shape, known as a **double helix**.

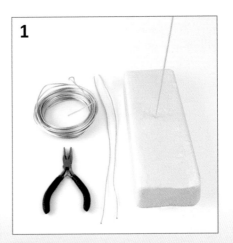

1

Step 1
Stick the skewer into the Styrofoam block. Use the wire cutters to cut two lengths of wire, each about 50 percent longer than the skewer.

2

Step 2

Gently bend the pieces of wire into spiral-shaped curves. On either side of the skewer, push the wires into the base, about 1 inch (2.5 cm) away from it, so that they spiral around it.

3

Step 3

Now thread the Styrofoam balls and beads onto the wires in an alternating pattern. On each wire, put a ball, then a bead, then a ball, and so on, until they are fully covered.

4

Step 4

Cut the pipe cleaners into short sections about 3 inches (8 cm long). Cut the straws into sections about 1 inch (2.5 cm) long. Arrange the straw pieces into two groups, each containing two colors.

5&6

Step 5

Take a piece of pipe cleaner and thread two different-colored pieces of straw onto it from one of the piles. Push one end of the pipe cleaner into one of the Styrofoam balls at the bottom of the model.

Step 6

Wrap the pipe cleaner around the wooden skewer between the two pieces of straw. Push the other end of the pipe cleaner into the Styrofoam ball on the other side.

7

Step 7

Continue adding steps of the ladder in the same way until you reach the top. Make sure you always pair the same sets of two colors together, alternating the pairs each time.

DNA

The shape and structure of DNA is very important. The two sides of the "ladder" can separate, and collect new parts to make two new matching copies of the DNA. This is how DNA is copied when cells divide, and when new cells, seeds, or babies are made.

Adenine, cytosine, guanine, and thymine are four chemicals known as bases, which make up part of the structure of DNA.

STRUCTURE OF DNA

Adenine

Cytosine

Guanine

Thymine

Base pairs (the ladder "rungs")

Double helix

Separated strand

FABULOUS FOSSILS

Make a realistic-looking fossil, **or create your own imaginary fossil creature!**

MARY ANNING

(1799–1847)

Mary Anning was a British fossil collector and paleontologist (fossil scientist). Near her home in Lyme Regis, England, she discovered important fossils, including those of the sea reptiles, ichthyosaur and plesiosaur, and a flying reptile called a pterosaur. Anning was also a skilled artist, making detailed drawings of her discoveries in order to share information about them with other fossil experts. Paleontologists of the time also made plaster casts of fossils, so that they could transport, display, and study the models without damaging the original.

This is a cast of the skull of one of the ichthyosaurs (sea reptiles) that Anning discovered.

WHAT YOU NEED

- items to cast, such as small fossils, seashells, bones, or teeth
- old newspapers
- lots of plasticine
- a stone that is mostly flat, smaller than the plasticine
- plaster of Paris
- measuring cups
- a large yogurt or ice cream tub that is empty and clean
- a wooden skewer or a craft stick
- petroleum jelly or baby oil
- paints (optional)

Step 1

Shape your plasticine into a slab about 1.5 inches (4 cm) thick. Make sure your stone is clean, then rub it with petroleum jelly or baby oil. Press it firmly into the plasticine, then carefully lift it out.

Step 2

Take the item you want to cast, such as a shell. Press it into the middle of the indentation made by the stone, then pull it out. It will leave a print of its shape behind. You can make several different molds, if you have enough plasticine.

Step 3

Spread out newspapers to work on. Measure one cup of water, and pour it into the yogurt or ice cream tub. Add 1.5 cups (360 mL) of plaster of Paris, and stir gently with the skewer or stick to make a creamy mixture.

Step 4

With an adult's help, pour plaster of Paris into your molds, filling them to the top. Leave them to harden for at least one hour. Then carefully peel away the plasticine to reveal the fossil casts.

Step 5

Leave the casts for a few more hours to dry out completely. If you like, you can then paint them in grayish-brown colors to look like real stone.

FOSSIL FORMATION

Fossils themselves are a kind of cast. They can form when objects like bones or shells are trapped under layers of sand or mud that slowly harden into rock. The bone or shell eventually dissolves away, leaving a space in the rock that is filled with stony **minerals**.

Paleontologists dig up fossils of ancient living things, millions of years after fossils form.

MAGICAL CREATURES

To make a mysterious magical fossil, make a tiny mermaid, unicorn, or dragon skeleton from clay. When it's hard and dry, use it to make a fossil cast.

GLOSSARY

algae A group of plant-like living things, including pond slime and seaweed, that grow mostly in water

animate To create a movie or film from a series of still images, such as photographs or drawings

anthocyanin A red, purple, or blue pigment found in some plants

bacteria A type of tiny living thing that can be seen using a microscope

biology The study of life and living things

breed To cause living things, such as dogs, to reproduce or have babies

carbon dioxide A gas that is produced by some types of living things

cells The small units that make up living things

chlorophyll A green pigment found in plants that takes in energy from sunlight

condense To change from a gas into a liquid

DNA The double helix-shaped material in cells that stores information about the characteristics and function of living things

double helix A shape similar to a ladder twisted into a spiral

ecosystem A community of living things together with their nonliving physical environment

entomologist A scientist who studies insects

evaporate To change from a liquid into a gas

fossil The bones or imprint of something that was once alive, preserved in rock

fungi A group of living things that includes mushrooms, molds, and yeast

indigo A blue dye made from indigo plants

instinct A skill or impulse that an animal is born with

lens A curved, transparent object used to make light bend, or refract, as it passes through it

life cycle The series of changes a living thing goes through as it is born, grows up, and has its own young

minerals Pure, nonliving substances found in nature, such as iron or quartz

oxygen A gas found in the air that animals need to breathe in order to survive

paleontologist A scientist who studies fossils and the history of life on Earth

pigment A natural coloring, especially one found in a living thing

pupa An insect in the stage of development between a larva and an adult insect

sound waves Waves of vibrating molecules that travel through a medium, such as air or water

species The scientific name for a particular type of living thing

stethoscope A device used to listen to sounds in the body

terrarium A clear enclosed container for keeping plants or other living things alive inside

turmeric A yellow spice used as a dye or to flavor food

water cycle The series of stages that water goes through as it moves between the sky, the sea, and the land

zoopraxiscope An invention that showed moving images before the movie projector was invented

FURTHER INFORMATION

WEBSITES ABOUT LIVING THINGS

Science Kids: Biology
www.sciencekids.co.nz/biology.html

National Geographic Kids: Dino Death Pit
www.kids.nationalgeographic.com/explore/
science/dino-death-pit/#trex.jpg

Smithsonian Science Education Center: Habitats
www.ssec.si.edu/habitats

Smithsonian Science Education Center: Insects
www.ssec.si.edu/expedition-insects

WEBSITES ABOUT MAKING

American Museum of Natural History: Create a Coral Reef
www.amnh.org/explore/ology/
marine-biology/create-a-coral-reef2

Arkive: Animal Activities
www.arkive.org/education/activities#shoebox-habitats

Exploratorium: Designer Ears
www.exploratorium.edu/snacks/designer-ears

WHERE TO BUY MATERIALS

The Home Depot
For pipes, tubing, wood, glue, and other hardware
www.homedepot.com

Michael's Stores
For art and craft materials
www.michaels.com

BOOKS

Hyde, Natalie. *Dinosaur Fossils*. Crabtree Publishing, 2014.

Lawler, Janet. *Scary Plants!* Penguin Young Readers, 2017.

Levete, Sarah. *Maker Projects for Kids Who Love Animation*. Crabtree Publishing, 2016.

Romero, Libby. *Insects*. National Geograhpic, 2017.

Stuckey, Rachel. *Energy From Living Things: Biomass Energy*. Crabtree Publishing, 2016.

PLACES TO VISIT

The American Museum of Natural History
www.amnh.org

National Museum of Natural History, Washington, DC
www.si.edu/museums/natural-history-museum

Canadian Museum of Nature
www.nature.ca/en/home

Chicago Field Museum, Chicago, USA
www.fieldmuseum.org

INDEX

animals 4–5, 9–10, 14–19
Anning, Mary 28–29
art 5, 18–19, 22–25, 28

bacteria 4, 7, 9
book, flip 16–17
brains, human 4, 17
bug viewer 14–15

carbon dioxide 7
casts 22–25, 28–29
cells, living 4, 13, 26–27
creepy-crawlies 14–15
Crick, Francis 26

DNA 4, 26–27
dinosaurs 28
doctors 20–21
double helix 26–27
dyes, natural 10–13

ecosystems 5, 7
entomologists 14

Fabre, Jean-Henri 14–15
fabric dying 10–13
film 5, 8–9, 16–17
films, time-lapse 8–9
fossils 28–29

genes 26–27
Gormley, Antony 22

hearts, human 20–21
humans 4–5, 16–17, 20–25

ichthyosaurs 28
India 10
insects 6, 9, 14–15
installations, art 18–19

Jonke, Sven 18

Katzler, Christoph 18

Laennec, René 20–21
lenses 14–15

molecules, DNA 26–27
Muybridge, Eadweard 16–17

Numen/For Use 18–19

Ott, John 8–9
oxygen 7

paleontologists 28–29
photography 5, 8–9, 16–17
photos, time-lapse 8–9
pigments, plant 13
plants 4–13

Radeljković, Nikola 18

sculptures 5, 22–25
species 4
spiders 18–19
stethoscopes 20–21

terrarium 6–7
tie-dye 10–13
tree of life 4

Ward, Nathaniel Bagshaw 6–7
Wardian cases 6–7
water cycle 7
Watson, James 26
waves, sound 21
webs 18–19

zoopraxiscopes 16–17